MORNING EARTH

ALSO BY JOHN CADDY

THE COLOR OF MESABI BONES
EATING THE STING
PRESENCES THE BLOOD LEARNS AGAIN

MORNING EARTH
FIELD NOTES IN POETRY

JOHN CADDY

MILKWEED
EDITIONS

© 2003, Text by John Caddy
© 2003, Interior art by R.W. Scholes
All rights reserved. Except for brief quotations in critical articles or reviews, no part of this book may be reproduced in any manner without prior written permission from the publisher: Milkweed Editions, 1011 Washington Avenue South, Suite 300, Minneapolis, Minnesota 55415. (800) 520-6455 / www.milkweed.org / www.worldashome.org

Published 2003 by Milkweed Editions
Printed in the United States of America
Cover and interior design by Christian Fünfhausen
Interior art by R.W. Scholes
The text of this book is set in Hoefler.
03 04 05 06 07   5 4 3 2 1
First Edition

Milkweed Editions, a nonprofit publisher, gratefully acknowledges support from the Bush Foundation; Joe B. Foster Family Foundation; Furthermore, a program of the J. M. Kaplan Fund; General Mills Foundation; Jerome Foundation; Dorothy Kaplan Light; Lila Wallace-Reader's Digest Fund; Marshall Field's Project Imagine with support from the Target Foundation; McKnight Foundation; Minnesota State Arts Board through an appropriation by the Minnesota State Legislature; National Endowment for the Arts; Kate and Stuart Nielsen; Deborah Reynolds; St. Paul Companies, Inc.; Ellen and Sheldon Sturgis; Surdna Foundation; Target Foundation; Gertrude Sexton Thompson Charitable Trust; James R. Thorpe Foundation; Toro Foundation; United Arts Fund of COMPAS; Lois Ream Waldref; Brenda Wehle and John C. Lynch; and Xcel Energy Foundation.

Library of Congress Cataloging-in-Publication Data

Caddy, John.
    Morning earth : field notes in poetry / John Caddy.—1st ed.
        p.   cm.
    ISBN 1-57131-416-4 (pbk. : alk. paper)
    1. Nature—Poetry.   2. Seasons—Poetry.   I. Title.
    PS3553.A313 M67 2003
    811'.54—dc21

                                        2002152809

This book is printed on acid-free paper.

THIS BOOK, AS ALWAYS,
FOR MY LIFE'S COMPANION, LIN

MORNING EARTH

Acknowledgments

I gratefully acknowledge the support, monetary and emotional, of Jill Goldesbury and the Stanley Foundation; Anna Barker and Wilder Forest; Tracy Fredin and John Shepard of the Center for Global Environmental Education at Hamline University in St. Paul, Minnesota; Emilie Buchwald, Hilary Reeves, Elizabeth Cooper, Laurie Buss, and Christian Fünfhausen and everyone else at Milkweed Editions for editing and creating this book; Chris Johnson and the Ojai, California, schools; Randall Scholes; Debra Fraser for unwavering grace; Jeff Prauer and the staff of COMPAS; Mary Altman; Bert Biscoe, poet of Cornwall; Owen Caddy, naturalist and writer; Kelly Finnerty and the Childrens' Museum of St. Paul; all the teachers who have shared the Earth Journal with their students; and not least the Earth Journal subscribers, past and present, whose response has been invaluable. To all, a heartfelt "Thank you!"

About Earth Journaling

My Earth Journal is a celebration of Earth's daily gifts. For me it is a daily daybreak practice—if you will, a devotional practice—a way of integrating myself with the whole of life. It lets me know each day that I belong to something infinitely larger and older than myself. It is a path to intimacy with nature and an awareness that we are the conscious part of Earth. We are Earth regarding itself.

My Earth Journal is a celebration of place, the piece of land where I live. My task as a poet is to share my experience of my home ground. Sharing the poems is an essential communal act.

I write each dawn and email the resulting entry to several hundred readers on four continents. Many readers are teachers, who share the entries with students each day.

Our task is to embrace nature in its particulars. We can connect to this tree, that chipmunk, this green iridescent beetle more easily than we can love an abstraction called Nature. The problem is, these days most of us have little experience with the living world. A daily poem about local wild doings is my way of trying to increase that experience. In forty years of teaching children and adults to write poetry, I have been amazed at how powerful their writing becomes when it turns to lives other than human and to environments other than urban. There is an inherent biophilia in us; we are fundamentally attracted to the rest of living nature.

The Earth Journal is about context. The broadest context is the biosphere, the skin of life that envelops Earth. The study of how the biosphere works is ecology. Ecologists teach us that everything is connected and interdependent. We commonly repeat this, but often don't grasp it. We can't grasp it without placing our persons in it. We don't just inhabit the biosphere, we belong to it; human life is one of its processes. Earth Journal writing requires close observation of process, not just of events, to learn how lives and forces intertwine. My comments after the poems in this book serve to place the poems in their natural context.

Sharing work that is raw can be frightening, but I have found readers to be consistently generous. My intent in writing and sharing without pause is partly to demystify poetry; the elevated mystique around creating poetry is a barrier to many who would like to write but have been sold a lot of nonsense. So my daily emails are presented warts-and-all.

One of my goals with the Earth Journal is to practice a transparent poetry that is simple and accessible. People respond to it, I suspect, because we all hunger for news of Earth and reassurance that the wild exists. My hope is that the Earth Journal helps readers and students know they are part of the community of life, from which our culture often divorces us.

If what you read in the following pages encourages you to celebrate in words the natural earth, you will find doing so deeply worthwhile. At the end of *Morning Earth,* I offer a few pages of suggestions for such writing.

MORNING EARTH

The Way

Go out into Earth.
Roll in moss, lick a pebble,
dance a circle round a tree, catch
a falling feather on your palm,
watch a turtle head thumb up
from pond to measure you—
smile greeting,
for this going out is going in,
in to your root nature,
for you are Earth, and if you are
to know yourself, you must know
the rest of Earth, and know too
that each atom of your flesh has been
since Earth has been,
and always has been shared
with all alive, and know as well
how in each live cell the spirals dance,
as spiraled stardust coalesced
into the sun and Earth

and eventually you,
for going out is going in.

John Muir said once in a letter that "going out, I found, was really going in." Now, a century and a half later, we explore this truth as ecopsychology.

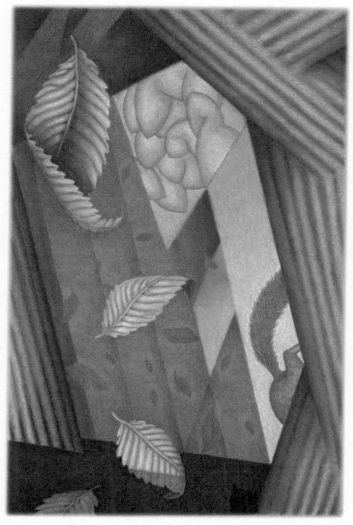

FALL

September 4

Turtleheads just in bloom.
I brush my hand through buds,
come back with a large treefrog
placid in my palm.
I have not felt her enter, but now
light green vibrates in my skin,
belly cool as last night's moon.
Legs neatly tucked, she's in no rush,
lets me lift her to my sight,

her eyes incurious, gold and black.
On her sides she mimics lichen,
ragged green-gray patches, white edged here,
there bright orange. On tree bark, her back would turn
all lichen gray, but here on turtleheads
she is utter leaf, her skin a thousand

tiny beads, each gleaming green.
She shifts a cool leg. I lower her to leaves.

Getting close is usually difficult. This calm treefrog against my skin was an incredible gift. Cherish moments when a wild life touches you without fear.

September 20

The white horse lets me caress his face,
enormous bone behind his skin,
this great round of jaw.
I rub between his ears,
slide down and stroke his nose.
He whuffs out at me:
hot air from a bellows wide.

*Touch other lives as you can. When a cousin of any kind
allows me touch, I am honored. One way to ensure our
humanity is to caress lives that are not themselves human.*

September 21

Light breeze,
a greengold curled leaf falls,
catches on a twig, becomes
a sudden warbler.

Earth presents us images continually. The small single-image poem is the root of poetry. Experiencing the image begins a process. Translating the image into words requires you to express its personal impact, its subtle influence. The end of the process is a shareable healing.

September 24

A perfect morning mushroom
swells from roadside grass.
It grows broad and domed, a stool
for royalty of toad.
Its color fawn,
its texture suede,
its temperature amphibian,
it is the autumn apple of Earth's
hidden streams, soon ripe-ribbed
with spores below the parasol
now opened to the fine rain
that sent perfection swelling out of soil.

*Ephemeral as mayflies, mushrooms are as sudden. They are
ambiguous, the fruit of soil, fed by decay, spawned by rain.
Tolerate, even celebrate, your own ambiguities, as I celebrate
the lovely lowly toadstool.*

September 25

Warm fall winds
rustle cattails, sigh grasses dry.
Sulfur butterflies lollop down fields,
let breeze take them, uncurl
tongues to taste red clovers,
asters, tall clovers white.

Paused fold-wing, one sulfur
tumbles a golden primrose,
another sails from a clover head
and spots the first, then in flight
with delicate antenna just

strokes the first,
so both leap fluster up
to quick-taste other, as quickly part
to catch the breeze away.

This quick dance bobs the paths of lives:
to taste the other before the cold,
so briskly wind does sweep us fluttering along.
The tasting makes the dance.

*Consider moments when all depends on whether a brief touch
stops at the reaching out or completes itself.*

October 3

Off the trail a yellow aspen leaf
spins on a spider silk
spins with the breeze
without sound
blinks light
winks bright
twice
each round

The leaf entirely captured me. There was a shock at how much resonance this spinning leaf contained. Days later it still ripples in my mind. When images persist, cast them into words as you would cast a spell.

October 11

The rounded heads of oaks roll across the woods,
some still stubborn green, most
washed bright with color.
They have lifted earth into themselves,
the mineral colors pulled up the roots,
up the trunk and down the veins of leaves.
Here red ocher, umber, yellow clay.
There a whole wide tree of burnt sienna glows.

*Writing reveals things we didn't know we knew. Trees really
do lift earth into themselves. Here the images connect the
painter's palette to autumn's larger palette. Connect your
human life to nature's lives. We are natural beings.*

October 12

In today's rebirth of summer sun
a shaggy mane mushroom juts from the lawn,
its tall white cone swells toward parasol.
On the tip is perched a mourning cloak
who slowly fans her wings, open, close, open
in brown and blue, yellow and black,
dark with a line of bright, open, close, . . .

*The butterfly does not know it will soon die. But nature is
our mirror. When Earth gives us images that reflect what is
going on inside ourselves, we find real connections to our own
lives, for we are the earth made conscious, able to reflect on
what we experience. That is our great gift.*

October 18

As I watch leaves
fall from trees,
I become incredibly aware
that air is really there,

that even in this windless
autumn daydream,
air in its own reverie
eddies like a stream,
slides a leaf this way, that,
then spins it down to ground

to sink into soil and wait
to be pulled up by roots again
to dance in the air
that really is there.

It is astonishing to suddenly realize something you have always known or been told. Received knowledge must become experience before it can be true.

October 19

A pair of redtails are skreeling down the sky,
calling again and again from so high
they are lost now and then to my eyes.
Odd to know they see me lurching down the road
with their hawk vision made
for pinning voles and rabbits to the grass.
Now they do not hunt, they play
in circles crossing, almost touching,
catching updrafts, lazing lower,
crying out again in pleasure of the sky.

*Everyone plays, behaviorists be damned. Find every
connection that you can between your own life and other
animal lives.*

October 20

Most freeze quietly, but not the paper wasps.
By afternoon, when the angled sun is warm,
they bump and bump against the windows,
long legs dangling, looking for a crack
to burrow deep.
Their urgency is old as time,
to keep their kind alive.
Most will freeze.
The clever will survive.

Sometimes the gifts Earth offers us are gifts not of joy, but of learning. Learning often hurts, but such learning is a kind of joy delayed.

October 24

The young red squirrel
sits up, forepaws tight to breast,
tail folded snug up to her back,
fur recurved at tail tip.
Her reds release light.

From her repose, her long hind foot
taps twice and stills,
taps twice and stills.
Her toes are delicate and clawed.
The line where white breast
meets red back is sharp and fine.
Nothing moves. A breeze stirs tail tip.
Her hind foot
taps twice and stills,
taps twice and stills.

What is going on here I cannot know. But I do know kinship. This foot tap charms my own moveable toes. Enjoy mysteries for themselves.

October 26

A milkweed pod
flowers its silk onto the wind.
The pebble-skin yawns, white
billows from the center,
a gust looses floss, the first flight
of seeds ride their silks
already high and free,

off to feed caterpillars
and turn them into kings—

what the wind is for.

*Those plants that rely on wind to spread their seed are the
pioneers that green disturbed ground, that prepare the soil for
a second species group. Succession on scraped ground is Earth's
green bandage.*

November 1

All day south wind.
The cattails rustle in their blades,
long grasses whisper fluently as rain.
Up close, thin ticks of dry collisions.

The long wind speaks in other tongues,
the roar of trees across the road,
the clatter of a distant grackle swarm.

On the edge of the cattail marsh
a deerbed's flattened grasses
silent as if under snow.

All these auguries and signs prepare us for winter's grip.
November winds make a lovely music out of all this dying
back.

November 2

Leaves down
Red apples heavy
on the bare tree

Tonight
Silver apples
of the moon

All is transformed by the light that bounces off the full moon.
Such poignance in the unattended harvest.

November 7

Two sets of tracks along the roadside,
the buck's on the south, dewclaw-deep and wide,
doe's along the north. Both walk
toward the sunrise hinted in the sky.

Say this tale I tell myself is true.
Say these two walk night together
but apart. She walks ahead of him,
places hind hooves exactly in her front tracks,
elegant perfuming.

The nostrils of both wet and wide,
ears cocked. Breeze from south,
she scents him first, and strolls.
When he scents her he cuts a quick scrape
with his hind hooves—here—
throws his antlers back, coughs loud.

She stops, all ears and lifted nose.
Say you tell the rest.

Reading sign is a way of taling time. Tracks are flashback stories that are sometimes clear, sometimes obscure. We are one of the few critters that worry about covering their tracks. When you notice tracks, read them back.

November 26

In a snowy field
three juncos feed.
Their weight curves down
the stalks of weeds
as they pluck the fuel
the fire needs.

Small winter birds are so intent and clear, they continually astonish. In these juncos' minds there is nothing going on except Eat these seeds. *The fire is no metaphor. The cellular processes that give all lives energy are in fact combustion.*

WINTER

December 2

On the deck
catprints in the frost
wait for sun's eraser.

Simple gifts suggest clear and simple expression. Write directly from experience and stay within the moment as you write. Bashō, the haiku master, once asked, "Is there any good in saying everything?"

December 11

On this blue-sky bright December day,
sprinkled like huge peppercorns
amid tree trunks on the white floor,
twenty wild turkeys crouch on snow,
heads tucked into feather down,
black wings folded large.
They all face north, source of bitter cold,
backsides to the winter sun,
blacksides to the winter sun.

*Sometimes the best survival strategy is to hunker down,
stay quiet, and absorb what you can. Imagine how very long
turkeys have been relying on solar heating to live through
bitter cold.*

December 19

Their broad backs steaming white,
already they have rolled
in crystals fresh fallen
from the circling sky turned blue
for them this spreading day.

Black horses toss their heads and race
thunder down the field,
kick powder into light, rear and chase,
cavort like colts,
and my feet yearn to flow into
this pure horseplay at ten degrees below.

*When adult animals of any kind frolic as they did when new,
especially under a blue sky, the earth rejoices. Fresh fallen
snow is opportunity for expressing joy of life.*

December 22

This long-night solstice sky is filled with fires
that burn through air so cold
on this small northern place
of tilted Earth, air so cold
it carries echoes of the void,
the heatless absolute of space,

yet these ancient stars
are the memories of fires
that burned long before eyes
ever tilted up to them
and thought of light.

*Understanding requires context. The enormous scale of time
and space gives us a perspective with long eyes.*

January 4

Open to the cold
on the surface of the snow,
breaths inhaled are knives
and exhaled breaths are frozen clouds.

But the way of Earth provides:
life is warmer under snow
where tunnels criss and cross.
Life below is safe from hawk
and owl, but under snow,
life can be fierce.

Shrew hunts meat in darkness
driven by his racing heart.
Ermine, sinuous and long,
ripples through white tunnels
disguised herself as snow,

sniffing after mouse and vole.
For all, the way of Earth provides.

All lives survive on what other lives provide. Energy transfers from life to life. Look beyond narrow human concerns and become aware of our intricate interdependence.

January 10

She sits a branch ten feet from me,
tail S curved, sweet breakfast
held between her fine forefeet
while she chisels meat from shell.
Done, she wipes her paws,
strokes her cheeks, abruptly
races down the trunk into her tunnel
under snow to find
another acorn for another treat.

Take your time. Beauty and complex relationships often reveal themselves slowly, blurred at first but coming clear as you get closer. Everything on Earth has a story to tell. Quiet all your busyness and be still long enough to hear a little of the stories being told.

January 18

Eight below
Crisp new snow
Sun up ice-haloed
Caw of crow

The gifts of Earth are simple things; reflect that in your writing. Use small clear words where you can.

January 22

As sky begins to glow, a barred owl
sits a hoarfrost branch and looks around,
around, and all the other way around,
a pair of hungry eyes perched upon a swivel,
but mostly he is feathered ears:
he hears the tiny sounds
of mouse claws on the crystal snow
where tunnels end and day is risked for food.
Owl's hunt is so still that when I see a talon flex
I almost hear long hoarfrost crystals
break and sift to ground.

Observation, like any hunt, is done with all the senses.
Practice being still. Stillness is a more attractive idea than
being quiet, or listening. If you become very still within
yourself, you will open to the world outside yourself.

January 23

In the pond, minnows hang
suspended in their peaceful sleep,
pectoral fins slightly fanning now and then,
light slowed from above by ice and snow
but present as a waterglow
that passes through the calm flesh
of transparent minnow fry
that wait the winter out to grow.

*Cast out your observing imagination and net awareness of
the other lives around you. Fish beneath the ice really do
spend the winter hanging out, allowed by a lower metabolic
need. The pure wonder of all these lives so unlike our own!*

January 25

Through light morning fog
a possum sifts snow for something she can eat.
Her ears are hairless pink, ridged black
on edges where they froze one night.
Her pink tail tip has frozen off as well,
its end frostbite black. But here she is,
stubborn supple hands sifting snow in fog
the funky white of her wide possum back.

Life and seasons bite parts of us away. But each stubborn life insists on making do with what is left. Honor this universal persistence wherever you may find it.

February 7

In leaf litter under snow, the small
woodfrog would gleam with ice
if sunlight glowed so deep.
His raccoon mask is fixed
and hard as painted stone,
for he has become both life and ice.
The eyes are closed, the mouth line
grins at the trick this frog has played
on the winter of the world,
for wake he will from cold
and hop bright eyed through woods, slowed
at first but gleaming with a frog's fine living glow.

*Nurture a sense of wonder (astonishment!) at the incredible
mysteries of life on Earth. Life finds ways to stay alive.*

February 20

Earth has spent day after day
swallowing light
from the cold blue bowl of sky,
photon packets bouncing about
in crystals of white
and up into our eyes.
In spite of Siberian air
we drink down this bright
gift that speaks more each day of green
and less of ice.

*In some psychological terminus of winter, light enters our
eyes as boundless possibility and promise. We are amazed year
upon year.*

February 22

The snow has melted away
from where the doe had lain,
the doe a truck flung into drying cattails.
Melted away from where
for days I watched her disappear last fall.

How strange.
She was whitetail doe, mother of fawns.
Then with a truck's one quick blow
she was carcass, carrion for crows.

At autumn's end I saw still
her hair and bones, forelegs
and dark polished hooves,
white skull, long spine.

And now the snow has gone
and with it every trace of doe.
Earth slowly melted her,

took her back to roots sure
as sun quickly warmed this snow,
and lifted it away.

*Needless death is hard, but nothing is wasted. Every speck
of every body is recycled and used again. We all eat and are
eaten.*

February 27

From yesterday
I'll keep the broken goldenrod
that swings its gray head side to side
and rasps itself away against snow.

From this morning's dark I'll keep
the crack and creak of weight on planks
and the squeak of boots on snow
at twenty degrees below.

From this leap of light
I'll keep one crow
beating audible wings
into a world of wind-carved snow.

*Sense images are the threads we weave our memories from.
We can't really know which we will retain, but decision
channels energy.*

SPRING

March 2

A pair of redtails draws great wheels
through a sky so blue it aches,
one bird with breast of white,
the mate with breast of dark.
They sway downwind on
paths their stretching wing tips find
and row back up, three beats, two,
swerve into a current,
and then, for joy, careen right down the sky.
One dark, one white.

*Our dream of flight is never more poignant than when
watching the effortless great soarers discover a thermal and
own the sky. And the mutual play of this dissimilar pair!*

March 5

Snowflakes build up in windrows on the ground
like clouds of cottonwood fluff.
These clumped flakes of snow
so slowly fall they seem to lift and fly
as if native to the air.
These flakes are air's familiars.
This crystal rain has fallen
down through air a million times before,
fallen everywhere.
This water was once breathed by jellyfish
in the Sargasso Sea, once jetted from a squid,
once inside a tidal wave that overswept Atlantis,
fell as rain in West Australia
and was caught on dancing children's tongues.
This melting ice I've just licked from sleeve
has pumped through countless hearts
and soon may pump through mine.

All Earth has shared this water circling
in its dance through space and time.
Even has it been before these
slowly falling flakes of snow.

*The rhythm of the dance is central to our participation in
the flow of life on Earth. Every molecule of water in your
blood has already danced down every river of the world and
has rolled for centuries in ocean waves. Each molecule has
been locked in glacier ice for eons and has melted out to flow,
eventually, in you.*

March 13

This dawn, redpoll finches feed
as the east burns gold.
The great living globe of fire ignites
the red caps and ripe beaks
of these little fires
as they fuel the travel north again
to the place of birth
to pass the fire on.

*Microcosm/macrocosm is one of our oldest tools for thinking.
Discover the stream of similarities that flow between the
large and the small. Find and celebrate those connections. Pass
the fire on.*

March 18

I lift a colored pebble to my eye—a pebble wet
with melted snow, and bright.
My face lifts up to
wild geese bugling as they fly,
a song sung out the throat of Time.

How old? How far is sky?
This bugle cry has rung in human ears
and lifted human hearts and eyes
in this valley for ten thousand years,
since glaciers rubbed this pebble smooth, and died.

*Synchronicity fosters intuitive leaps; it demonstrates that all
really is connected. Earth is a fine tutor.*

March 21

Geese are bowing in the pond,
each to each, bowing low,
asking with their curved necks.
Behind them wood ducks pose
in the splendor of their feathers, all
reflected in the morning mirror where
for the ten-thousandth year
geese are bowing in the pond.

Develop a sense of deep time. Think about how long the actions you observe have been repeated on this Earth. The goal is to know something of what life is, what we are, to what we are connected, and from where we've come.

March 23

Two mallards arrow down
upon the mirror pond,
the water rolls the arrow-wake
in liquid silver for a moment,
smoothes reflected birches.
Ice is three days gone,
and six feet under silver,
painted turtles start to blink.

*Try to see beyond the surface. You will discover that you
already know what you need to know. Most learning in
ecology and art is not about "new" knowledge, but rather
about a process of bringing to awareness how much you
already intuit and know.*

March 24

This goldfinch male was winter pale.
Now longer days begin his change.
His breast begins to glow with yellow light,
beginning small, yet soon
he will pierce my eyes
like a splinter of the summer sun
and make them blur.

*The mating plumage of the birds is our aspiration. The
males are splendid and improbable. Males should always be
conscious that females do the choosing.*

March 28

Morning Earth speaks sweet
everythings in my ears:
rattle of woodpecker, thin chickadee,
warble of the jay, hoarse muted trumpets
from distant geese,
two big barking dogs,
squirrel scold, dove coo,
the tick of tiny paws.
Sandbagged again, goosebumped,
I can think only of Blake:
For every thing that lives is holy,
life delights in life.

How overwhelming is the whole, and what a wondered
waking. The amazing thing is that we're part of it, belong
to it.

March 31

All right, small friends.
Who ate the crocus down,
leaf and flower all?
Who ate the crocus right to ground?
What nibbler in the night
has such a taste for beauty?
Such a tooth so sweet for spring?

If a mouse pregnant with her first litter after winter decides my crocuses are delicious, should I rant? Or should I enjoy the fact that beauty can feed life in different ways?

April 3

In evening rain
black branches of a butternut
drop pearls into the pond.

As the soft rain tapers down
birches paint white
against dark glass again.

*Write directly and quickly from experience. Bashō said,
"When you are composing a verse, let there not be a hair's
breadth separating your mind from what you write. . . .
Never hesitate a moment."*

April 11

The rotting upright trunk is full of holes
the pileated woodpecker cut with his long beak,
holes carved wide and chiseled deep.
In the trunk I find a refuge, a hollowed place
where one small tough bird,
a chickadee or junco, put its back to winter wind
and to long winter night after winter night, leaving
droppings to tell the story now, in spring.
It left one gray feather there.

This little refuge gives me one:
that the woodpecker in its hunger
saved a life it neither knew about nor cared.
We live together here, and at times
we help without trying
by Earth's design.

Reading signs of life through time is a result of close seeing that enlarges us. Reading signs opens up a question box that ties us into other lives. Nature everywhere presents communities of living beings cooperating for mutual benefit. Intention is irrelevant. This symbiosis is fundamental to the ways life works.

April 13

In cold high air last morning,
a rainbow made of crystal ice and light
played ring-around-the-sun,

a diadem of every color circling gold
halo without end.

The disk enclosed was whitely cold
within the sky-bowl blue.

In this game of ring-the-sun
the rainbow's always open, always closed.

*When we write from nature observation, we find questions
more often than answers, and those questions pull us into our
existence.*

April 15

All night the dark ponds sing
of love and spring and all
that ripples in our oldest brain,
the song from throats that swelled
high-pitched before thunder lizards
wore the crown, long before
they cocked their heads and wondered
at spring ponds that sing.

Frog song is the ursong, a mother song that stirs up the porridge of our minds. What a marvel is the song of the frog. The singers here and now are chorus frog and wood frog and, for punctuation, the first peepers. How awful if we should still these first singers.

April 23

On a fresh-cut maple stump
cluster mourning cloaks.
The roots don't know the trunk is gone
and pump sweet sap into a pool
where spiral tongues uncurl
like New Year's party favors
and suck the sweet
to welcome their release.

*The stumped tree owns a blind vegetative insistence on
life that is both marvelous and fearful to us who are less
endowed. This stubborn desire is echoed by the mourning
cloaks, who celebrate their survival of six months of being
frozen by drinking wet sweets and minerals from the stump.
Life feeds on life and feeds on death. All is making and
unmaking. Nothing goes to waste.*

April 29

Trees are suddenly on flower:
catkins dangle green and gold, oaks
blush red, plums white, all abrupt
as the blush and bloom of puberty.
What magics push through stems
these sudden blooms
and the greening ears of leaves?

Suppose it is spring choirs:
the primal night song of the frogs,
the first-light chorus of the birds.
Say it's so.
Say the birds release the trees
while frog song greens plants close to soil—
old liverwort, mosses tossing spore caps,
berry bushes, lily thrust.

The choirs are fully throated now,
in these brief days when dawn-bright birds

overlap the night song of the frogs,
and all turns green and flowering,
and children almost know their loveliness.

Modern notions of causality are wanting. Mythically and metaphorically, leaf-green, spring flowers, and puberty are synchronous. Suppose cause is beside the point? Suppose being is central, and the flow of life and the nature of our participation in that flow is what matters?

April 30

In the dark just outside my window
something rushes up an oak like
a furry urgent inchworm, front legs first,
then the rear pulls humping up.
A pause, and out of sight.

Raccoon? Must be.
The tail is shorter in the dark, unringed.
What's up the tree? Only
a place he hasn't been.

In half a minute there he is again
with a different gait, smoothly
walking headfirst down the tree,
down the tree he has now seen,
down and out of sight.

Dark fills every night with animals intent on what we cannot see. This is their time, so many furry cousins that gather light with big round eyes. Raccoon eyes have shone in firelight here for twenty thousand years.

May 1

They surge north in waves each night,
and in the morning wake the forest floor
with hop-and-kick, as if fallen leaves
were gasping life. They know
that if they kick brown leaves enough,
bugs in plenty will turn up
to fuel night's beating wings.

At dawn they wake me into song
that threads me into reverie,
the whitethroat's whistle-song
that tomorrow will pierce
the taiga's heart and cry, "Again."

*The song of the white-throated sparrow evokes the north like
no other. It pierces deep, like the pipes or pennywhistle can. It
is a somehow Celtic song.*

May 3

Dry as a dragonfly wing
ladybird emerges from her winter crevice
in the kitchen cabinets, walks
slow across the counter-stone to sink,
where she strolls the rim
as I admire her colors,
bright as when she went to sleep. I hope
she doesn't see above her on the windowsill
a sister's husk, dome down, belly-up,
with tiny black legs clenched. She finds
the water drop I place before her. After,
we travel to the tulip bed, where
I trust she will be fed.

Encounters with tough little survivors evoke compassion, no matter the number of legs. We are in life one community, each with the same problems: water, food, a place to be. Generosity of spirit enlarges us.

May 6

Catkins set seed, past flowering,
as cattails spear green through
their own bleached wind-rattle bones.
High above her marshland nest
where every bush buds yellow-green,
the harrier knifes across the sky.
How on this wild wind against
slate sky she does slide flat out,
and out, and curves crosswind
behind the reddened tops of oaks.

*Soon, for a month, the harrier will fly only to catch the prey
her mate drops from the sky. She is so fierce as she incubates
that nothing living is allowed near her eggs.*

May 8

Orioles are blackbirds, by the book,
but flames of orange
burn open my snow-drabbed eyes.
Two pairs arrive, demand food, and receive
oranges, up from the tropics like themselves,
bright travelers well met upon my deck. Black beaks
plunge into halved oranges (I licked the cut sides first).
They eat orange sections in sequence, neatly
round the circle, one by one, and I again
eat grapefruit as a child,
from my mother learn to eat the sections
round the circle, one by one,
like these flaming blackbirds eat
the clock-face orange of sliced suns.

Orioles are so outrageously beautiful in spring that they are almost too much. Watching their sequenced way of eating oranges connects me to memories of my mother. Why on Earth would orioles eat orange sections in sequence? Delight in sweet rounds of mystery.

May 10

Cold gray skies, but jewels
everywhere.

On a thin branch
emerald fire—
a twist of his throat
and ruby burns.

Five hungry grosbeaks:
black and white,
brilliant rose.

Two orioles just in,
two beaks sunk deep
in orange halves.

Blackburnian warbler fires
abrupt orange head and breast.
His name is long, should be;

he's flown here from the Andes.
His tail sharp-scissors
black feathers, white.

*A glory of small morning birds has flown all night to be here.
It's thirty-four degrees and still these tough lives come. First
hummingbirds, first orioles, plus myrtle warblers headed
north and the bright striped heads of whitethroats. Mallards
dabble in the new ponds left from a four-inch rain. A whole
family of blue jays cavorts at bath. I am entirely honored.*

May 11

Cats on windowsills
chatter at the orioles on oranges
in voices piteous and plaintive
as carnivores can find.
Three tails lash intent.
They brim so with bird!

*Predators are so nourished by the moment, so incredibly
within the present that they show us a wholeness we
probably lost the moment we conceived of time. Our envy is
tinged with sadness, but we do find joy in the almost-memory
of being complete as a cat is complete.*

May 14

She bumbles into every window, hovers
before openings, crawls into cracks again, again,
until her palace place is found.
She is urgent and profound, for
within her abdomen, dynasties are quickening.
These sisters are no ordinary wasps.
They are young queens of May,
dangling gawky legs before us
until they find their place to lay.

*There is nothing more determined than a female searching
out a safe place to bear her children. For a paper wasp,
the first necessity is a hidden place where she can raise her
first workers. The wasp queen's urgency is connected to our
Maypoles and our Queens of May. Insect and mammal, all
dance within the same imperatives.*

May 15

A pair of mating dragonflies
bumbles awkwardly around the pond,
eight stiff wings engaged in birth.
The male's wings hold her just above the surface
as the tip of her abdomen dips below
and pulses eggs into the pond.
Then they lumber off to find another spot
around and round the pond.
I watch and every day see something
wonder-filled I've not seen before.

*This dragonfly behavior is intelligent: it maximizes egg
survival. But surely flies are not all that smart. So where
does this intelligence reside? It is the community, the eco-
system, that is bright. The inescapable conclusion is that all
of us live within intelligence.*

May 21

In bright sun,
the indigo bunting
flashes in,
lands on a white tulip,
bends it for a breath,
and flies.

Be careful when you look up, for you may be ambushed by joy. So much takes place in instants.

May 22

Plants thrust up from soil as if
from netherworlds, shapes strange
and all agleam with reds instead of green.
They are born to light wizened and
folded as a mammal babe
and as insistent to discover
light and to unfold.

*As the oak tops are red now before emerging leaves take
up their work, on the forest floor the blind urge toward
resurrection spears up again. Shades of the Green Man and
of Cadmus sowing dragon's teeth.*

May 23

The toads are in the pond
dangling from their golden eyes
while the throats of males swell
to fill the night with songs
antique before the dinosaurs.
The ancestors of song
now sing the pond and thrill
my still wet-behind-the-mammal-ears.

*Some beauties last. Grow a sense of deep time, for without
a temporal context we can't know who we are and where
we've been.*

SUMMER

June 1

Painted turtles play today
the oldest game in the pond:
"How Many Turtles Can Sun on a Log?"
As morning warms, each turtle claws
into day and finds a place to splay its legs
and stretch its neck out far.
As more turtles swim to the log to play,
they prop their shells upon the one before
until the whole turtle line is half upright
and flashing red plastron patterns,
a primal cancan strange and slow.
The answer by late afternoon today?
Twenty-One Turtles Can Sun on a Log.

*All the turtles want to do is warm themselves so they can
better digest their food. But this human observer finds their
solution to a crowded log marvelous.*

June 3

The wood thrush pours morning into me
like early light through basswood leaves,
a song that glows me out of bed.

Then pileated woodpecker cries out
his ululating almost-laugh,
gives me goosebumps on my joy,
wakes inside me all the wild.

*Sometimes it's hard to believe that these bird sounds have
nothing directly to do with me, for they affect me so. They
announce essential wildness in a way that evokes their
brilliant dinosaur past.*

June 6

Everything this morning wants to fly.

A stand of ferns, sunglowed, wings
feathered wide and sharp,
about to leap en masse and green the sky.

Maple fruits, samaras in full spiral flight
to Earth away from mother tree
on paper wings exactly shaped
to troll the winds.

Feel *samara* in your mouth.
There's a word to shape a soul for flight.

And I this morning wish to fly
beyond all words.

The magic of the air, the lift of the invisible. We have all danced in our hearts with seeds in flight. Who has not felt a pang when the seed grounds? Beyond romance, winged seeds had better fly far, or they will starve in mother's long shadow.

June 15

When the woods are wet with green
they sing with light that seems
to start inside each leaf,
each lichen on dark bark,
and glows into moist air
inhaled by every spiracle and lung
to make more breath for trees.

*The greens on rainy days are endlessly astonishing. Diffused
sunlight has no point source, so it really does seem to emanate
from every object seen.*

June 20

Blue jays come and go.
They know the sharpshinned hawk
wants sparrow, finch, or chickadee.

Sharpshin thinks he hides
inside the shrubs, but small birds
go to ground, sit still, and will not fly.

Small birds carry memories of ancient skies
inside their skulls. Sharpshin's shape, his yellow claw,
were carved into their brains a million years ago.

*Newborn iguanas panic at the sight of a boa but ignore a
garter snake. Species experience over unimaginably long
stretches of time does race the heart. So many questions come
back to Nature or Nurture.*

June 27

This land is what the glaciers spoke.
That hollow a vowel that took a century to gouge,
that lake uttered by a plunging waterfall,
this sandhill murmured by a stream
beneath a thousand feet of ice.

Glaciers spoke this land:
the slow grind of boulder teeth
growled simply, finally

ground.

*Here where the glaciers lived again and again, all the rocks
are round. Boulders are rubbed smooth. Sand grains are not
sharp. Our soils began in the mouths of ice. For long centuries
small animals lived within a ceaseless roar. Imagine the
moment it stopped.*

July 7

Yellow flowers depend from leaves
and scent the air with honey
while tumbling every bloom within the trees
a thousand humming bees
fill their legs with pollen,
tongue the nectar deep
as this sweet thrum of basswood trees.

You can hear the bees from a hundred yards and more in the
right breeze. It is astonishing that there are enough pollen
gleaners to tumble every leaf, bees intoxicated with purpose
fulfilled.

July 15

Trees create themselves
of water and of air,
as do you, as do I.

When the play is done,
into air we'll lift again,
into earth we'll sink.

*Trees and human beings are elaborations of carbon from
the air and hydrogen and oxygen from water, plus a few
dissolved gases and minerals. All substance is released at
death to nurture new life.*

July 17

Tearing off old bark from
dead standing trees I read
the sinuous tracks of beetle larvae
who carved these cryptic patterns,
who lived safe in here a life,

a journey eaten into wood,
here diving into dark,
there poking up, pushing before
the lovely sawdust of their chewing:
unread texts
beneath the bark of dying trees.

*Life is mystery. So much is written that goes unread. Look
beneath the bark.*

July 20

All winds on Earth
contain the caw of crow,
and all eyes the feathers black.
First the caw and then the crow
spread-fingered on swift air.
There is nowhere in the wind
that you can go
and not hear riding on it
caws of crows

whose minds are bright
as beads are bright as eyes
that watch the earth entire
and speak of it on bouncing
branches in crow-moots
every morning of the world

and take off into wind
and sail on down,

or beat against it, contrary crows
who are the caws
that ride the wind
wherever eyes can go.

Truly, crows are antic spirits, tricksters, Loki birds. And they are, as Mary Oliver says, "the deep muscle of the world."

August 5

The black dog trots across the road.
Something slack dangles from his jaws.
He's found some creature dead.
Tail held high, proud head,
he prances joy with all four paws.
He is so pleased I share his grin.
Joy lives where it will.

Imagination fails when we try to fathom how a dog's fabled nose can so delight in rotting flesh. We must take our cousins as they come.

August 16

On a forest floor, go to your knees.
Move aside dead leaves.
Trowel your fingers into soil
and lift some cupped before you, close.
Let your nostrils open wide.
What you smell has always been,
is then, is now, is when.
What you hold is all alive.
Your seven senses know it.
Look closely. Deep.

Nets on nets of threads connecting all.
This is Earth's placenta, this secret
densely woven lace that streams with life.
The threads are fungus roots that feed
each plant and tree upon this forest floor.
Each rootling of each plant expands by ten,
embraced by microscopic fungus tubes
that weave a web of food that flows

two ways: the plant is fed
with rock dissolved and water;
the fungus root is fed with light
the plant transforms with
water, air, and rock dissolved.

Now replace the mother earth.
Her nets will heal. Your hands have held
the moving crucible of life, and if you tremble,
well you should, for you are in it, of it,
living, here, where you will always be,
where you have always been.

*We are just beginning to grasp the crucial importance of
mycorrhizal symbioses. Almost all plants thrive only in
partnership with fungi. They have coevolved.*

August 17

Cardinal males so red
it's almost too much.

Cardinal females so richly
refined in their hues
I can't get enough.

*The most interesting beauty is subtle and reveals itself slowly,
or only at close range. It's like gradually learning the heart of
a friend.*

August 20

The green heron lifts his crest,
every feather on his head erect
as the snake dangles from his beak,
his yellow hunter's eye burns bright.
He stretches high his russet neck,
flips up his beak, and swallows long.
He folds his neck and crouches
just above the water on a branch,
and as his crest settles to his skull
his yellow hunter's eye burns bright.

*Predation is hard to watch but important; it stirs us up
in ancient ways. In the ecosystem, energy and matter
continually transfer from life to life, are always shared.
Without death, no life. But do feel for the snake, and feel the
mystery of intertwining life and death.*

August 21

Cicada song is belly drummed.
Since birth and burrowing,
nymphs buried long years
breathe and nibble roots and hear,
while hormones counsel patience,
the drum pulse of the earth.

At last en masse one night
huge nymphs dig out and hook to bark
and climb, then shudder from
the nymphal husks that pile up below
while freed adults caress new wings
into nets of cellophane.
What was buried is twice born.

The males fly a few feet to a branch
where they amplify the song
they learned from earth, they shrill it strong
from the tymbals in their bellies.

The females on their branches listen,
and when the song is overwhelming, fly to mate.

Cicadas listen to the song of earth.
Things rise out of earth and time
twice born, but not all sing,
not all have learned to hear the song.

*Subterranean grubs live for pale long years getting ready to
sing and respond. Great musicians prepare interminably for
that ultimate concert.*

August 24

The calico cat leaps again
to catch a sulfur butterfly,
once more claps her paws together
on the deepening sky.

*The blue of sky becomes deeper to the eyes as summer leans
into autumn. The sulfur of the butterflies complements the
grasses and cattails turning golden brown. So delighted is
the cat to play with butterflies that she applauds!*

August 30

Twin fawns watch me clump up the road, watch
a long time, take bites of branches
while they wait for me to cross the safety line
when they have to run. White tails flash up
and both fawns wheel in synchrony and run up the hill,
where they stand. Below them I stand,
all three of us still, looking. Both fawns
look at me over their shoulders,
necks curved in the sweet arc of wonder.

*There is no tensile curve like that of a grazer's neck. How
long have humans and the other natural beings been quietly
looking at each other when they meet?*

August 31

Speak to Earth, use your every voice,
speak to all her beings.
Praise the lives of green
and all the lives with legs.
Praise the lives who dance in air
and all who float and swim.
Praise the diggers and the delvers under soil.
Praise the spores and praise the seeds—
now close your eyes to see
the tiny wrigglers everywhere,
the simpler ones who came before.

When you greet a beetle on your hand,
your words praise Earth.
When you rescue from the street a woolly bear,
praise Earth with your chuckle from its feet.
When you lift your eyes to hawks,
your lilting heart is praise to Earth.

If we speak well to Earth,
she will fill our ears and eyes with secrets,
she will fill our dreams with healing images,
she will fill our hearts with joy to share.

Afterword

- In the introduction I said, "My Earth Journal is a celebration of place, the piece of land where I live." I would be delighted if some of my readers would commit to language some celebrations of their own home ground. It does not matter if you celebrate the silhouetted cactus or the glacial calving. What matters is that you become more intimate with the patch of Earth where you live. What matters is that you begin to perceive yourself within the context of your local ecosystems. If you can share the results, great! Your communal act will inspire others.

- The hard thing about writing is doing it. Many people think and talk about writing a lot, but rarely make words happen with their fingers. Writing is a physical act; it is not a thought process. Do not wait around for inspiration. Decide to write an entry a day, then do it. Decision is a way to gather energy.

- Begin writing from direct, momentary experience. Explore the intense moments your senses offer you. Do not start with ideas.

- Let your senses be intimate with life. Touch things, and be aware of textures. Taste the colors you are seeing. Close your eyes and hear.

- The joy of writing is surprise. Whenever you write, you surprise yourself by saying likable things that you did not plan. We are all filled with surprises. We all know more than we know. Writing is one way to let our knowing into the world.

- When poet William Stafford was asked what he did when he was blocked, how he got unstuck, he always replied, "I lower my standards." When you write, you are not required to be wonderful.

- Keep your writing simple. Don't be "poetic." Don't be fancy. Be clear, be simple, be accurate.

- You are a natural being. Include the human in your journal entries. If you exclude humanity from nature, you exclude your own deepest nature.

- Allow Earth to give you gifts. The gifts of Earth I celebrate include moments of beauty, intricacy, surprise, laughter, and learning.

- Accept the gift of learning, which may be painful to receive. From suffering and death we learn of life. From cruelty we discover the possibility of kindness. From the body of the bluebird frozen by storm we learn connection. From all of this we learn empathy.

- Don't require Nature to be Wilderness. Thoreau said, "In Wildness is the preservation of the World." Distinguish, as he did, between wildness and wilderness. We hunger for the wild. The wild is everywhere; it cannot be extinguished. The wild centers every seed, enters every garden. Wilderness is myth and gone, and the wild is everywhere. Wilderness is distant; wildness local. Wildness is the urge of life to *be*—the grass blade in the parking lot, the peregrine in the tower, weeds pioneering a landfill, the patch of brush where kids make forts.

- Be always willing to be surprised. Every day nature will show you things you have never noticed before.

- Be open. Before observing, try to empty yourself. Set aside your superficial concerns: schedules, aches and pains, nagging relationships, all that. Relax and be receptive. Be empty. Nature will fill you if you allow it.

- Listen to the stories Earth tells you. Every pine cone, every lichen, every leaf has stories you can learn to see and hear and share through writing.

- As you observe nature, be conscious of Deep Time. When katydids shrill on autumn nights, connect with the millions of years they've been singing. When you pick up a rounded pebble, know the thousand years it spent being rolled round by a glacial river. When a squirrel lashes you with its tail, imagine people in skins laughing at this same antic moment.

JOHN CADDY lives on ten acres of woods, ponds, and marsh near Forest Lake, Minnesota. John is descended from Cornish miners and grew up in iron mining towns on the Mesabi Range, surrounded by the North Woods. Both mine towns and forest have deeply informed his writing.

John has spent forty years teaching, as a resident poet for some seven hundred schools and as an instructor at Hamline University and the University of Minnesota. A Bush Artist Fellow, Caddy's poetry collections include *Eating the Sting* (Milkweed, 1986) and *The Color of Mesabi Bones* (Milkweed, 1989), which won the *Los Angeles Times* Book Prize and the Minnesota Book Award. He has read his poems nationwide and in England, most recently at the Eden Project.

Since 1994, John has been a stroke survivor and is hemiplegic. His focus since finding himself alive again has been to unite his two great loves: ecology and making poems. Caddy's Self Expressing Earth Internet Program at Hamline University has immersed many teachers, artists, and naturalists in learning ecology through making art. In Cornwall, in 2002, John was initiated as a Bard of the Cornish Gorseth. His bardic name is Kaner an Norvys, Singer of Earth.

MORE POETRY FROM

MILKWEED ◉ EDITIONS

To order books or for more information, contact Milkweed at
(800) 520-6455 or visit our website *(www.milkweed.org)*.

Turning Over the Earth
Ralph Black

Outsiders:
Poems about Rebels, Exiles, and
Renegades
Edited by Laure-Anne Bosselaar

Urban Nature:
Poems about Wildlife in the City
Edited by Laure-Anne Bosselaar

Drive, They Said:
Poems about Americans and
Their Cars
Edited by Kurt Brown

Night Out:
Poems about Hotels, Motels,
Restaurants, and Bars
Edited by Kurt Brown and Laure-
Anne Bosselaar

Verse and Universe:
Poems about Science and
Mathematics
Edited by Kurt Brown

Astonishing World:
Selected Poems of Ángel González
Translated from the Spanish by
Steven Ford Brown

Mixed Voices:
Contemporary Poems about Music
Edited by Emilie Buchwald and
Ruth Roston

This Sporting Life:
Poems about Sports and Games
Edited by Emilie Buchwald and
Ruth Roston

The Phoenix Gone,
The Terrace Empty
Marilyn Chin

Twin Sons of Different Mirrors
Jack Driscoll and Bill Meissner

Invisible Horses
Patricia Goedicke

The Art of Writing:
Lu Chi's Wen Fu
Translated from the Chinese by
Sam Hamill

Boxelder Bug Variations
Bill Holm

The Dead Get By with Everything
Bill Holm

Butterfly Effect
Harry Humes

Good Heart
Deborah Keenan

The Freedom of History
Jim Moore

The Long Experience of Love
Jim Moore

The Porcelain Apes of Moses
Mendelssohn
Jean Nordhaus

Firekeeper:
New and Selected Poems
Pattiann Rogers

Song of the World Becoming:
New and Collected Poems 1981–2001
Pattiann Rogers

White Flash/Black Rain:
Women of Japan Relive the Bomb
Edited by Lequita Vance-Watkins
and Aratani Mariko

Join Us

Since its genesis as *Milkweed Chronicle* in 1979, Milkweed has helped hundreds of emerging writers reach their readers. Thanks to the generosity of foundations and of individuals like you, Milkweed Editions is able to continue its nonprofit mission of publishing books chosen on the basis of literary merit—the effect they have on the human heart and spirit—rather than on the basis of how they impact the bottom line. That's a miracle our readers have made possible.

In addition to purchasing Milkweed books, you can join the growing community of Milkweed supporters. Individual contributions of any amount are both meaningful and welcome. Contact us for a Milkweed catalog or log on to www.milkweed.org and click on "About Milkweed," then "Supporting Milkweed," to find out about our donor program, or simply call (800) 520-6455 and ask about becoming one of Milkweed's contributors. As a nonprofit press, Milkweed belongs to you, the community. Milkweed's board, its staff, and especially the authors whose careers you help launch thank you for reading our books and supporting our mission in any way you can.

Interior design by Christian Fünfhausen
Typeset in Hoefler 11/15
by Stanton Publication Services
on the Pagewing Digital Publishing System.
Printed on acid-free 55# Sebago 2000 Antique Cream paper
by Maple-Vail Book Manufacturing.